America's Game
Seattle
Mariners

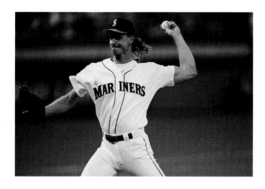

Paul Joseph

ABDO & Daughters
PUBLISHING

Published by Abdo & Daughters, 4940 Viking Dr., Suite 622, Edina, MN 55435.

Cover photo: Allsport
Interior photos: Wide World Photo, pages 1, 8, 9, 11, 12, 14, 15, 17, 21, 23, 24, 27

Edited by Kal Gronvall

Library of Congress Cataloging–in–Publication Data

Joseph, Paul, 1970-
    Seattle Mariners / by Paul Joseph
        p. cm. — (America's game)
    Includes index.
    Summary: Provides details of the history of the Seattle Mariners, a team that made its debut in 1977 and has yet to win the American League pennant.
    ISBN   1-56239-680-3
    1. Seattle Mariners (Baseball team)—Juvenile literature.
[1. Seattle Mariners (Baseball team)—History.   2. Baseball—History.] I. Title. II. Series.
GV875.S42J67 1997
796.357' 64' 09797772—dc20   96-23781
                                                                    CIP
                                                                    AC

Contents

Seattle Mariners 4

The Mariners Are Born 7

Inaugural Season 8

Wrong Turn 10

Still Building 11

Now What? 13

The Kid 14

The Griffeys Make History 15

What Happened? 20

Mariners' First Pennant 22

A Team On The Rise 27

Glossary 29

Index 31

Seattle Mariners

The Seattle Mariners' franchise had the hardest job in all of sports—starting an expansion franchise. When the team made its debut in 1977, Seattle fans knew that it would be awhile before they had a winner.

But it took a lot longer than most expected. It was 15 seasons before the Mariners had a season over .500, and it took almost 20 years before they won a division title. They are still waiting for that elusive American League (AL) pennant and a chance at winning the World Series.

Even worse, the Toronto Blue Jays, who came into the league as an expansion team the very same year as Seattle, have done so much better than the Mariners. Within 10 years the Blue Jays had won their division. By the time the Mariners had a winning season, the Blue Jays were on their way to back-to-back World Series Championships.

Facing page: Ken Griffey, Jr., smacks another ball out of the park during a game against the Oakland Athletics.

Now the tide has turned, and the Mariners are on the rise, while the Blue Jays are falling fast. In 1995, the Mariners won their first division title. They also took their first playoff series, and they fought hard in the American League Championship Series (ALCS), while the Blue Jays finished as the worst team in baseball.

With a talented crew led by two of the best young players in the league—Ken Griffey, Jr., and Alex Rodriguez—and a solid pitching staff led by ace Randy Johnson, the Mariners look like they will sail to the top of the league.

The Mariners Are Born

Before 1969, watching professional baseball in Seattle meant watching the Rainiers. The Rainiers were a minor league franchise in the Pacific Coast League. Many of their players went on to the major leagues.

Then in 1969, Major League Baseball arrived with the Seattle Pilots, an American League expansion franchise. The Pilots played only one year in Seattle before they began having financial difficulties. The bankrupt organization had to sell their team to a group that moved the Pilots to Milwaukee. The team was renamed the Brewers, and they began playing in Milwaukee in 1970.

For most of the 1970s, Seattle went without a major league team. Then, in 1976, the American League expanded, adding teams in Toronto and Seattle.

Seattle had a new domed stadium waiting for them. The Kingdome would be used for professional baseball and football.

After being awarded the team, the six investors who owned the Seattle franchise had to pick a name. After having a "Name That Team" contest, they chose the Mariners, which was picked from 15,000 contest entries.

The Seattle Mariners were officially born. Now the hard part began—getting players for this expansion franchise. They had less than one year to put together a Major League Baseball roster.

Inside the Kingdome on opening day, April 7, 1977. The Mariners lost to the California Angels 7-0.

Inaugural Season

The Mariners' organization had a plan. They were going to get a first-rate team by building a solid minor league system, selecting good draft choices, and making trades when needed. Everyone knew it would take time and energy before Seattle would be winners.

The Mariners hired Darrell Johnson as manager. Johnson was a former catcher who had led the Boston Red Sox to the pennant in 1975. His first job was the expansion draft.

The first player drafted by the Mariners was Ruppert Jones, a young outfielder who had played for the Kansas City Royals. Jones

was a fan favorite that first year, as chants of "Rupe! Rupe! Rupe!" thundered throughout the Kingdome.

During a game against the Baltimore Orioles, Ruppert Jones steals second base.

Pitcher John Montague, one of the few bright spots in the Mariners' 1977 opening season.

After putting together a team, it was time to hit the field. The Seattle Mariners played their first-ever game at the Kingdome on April 6, 1977. Diego Segui was the starting pitcher for the Mariners. It wasn't a good game for Segui or for the Mariners, as they were trounced 7-0 by the California Angels.

The season did not get any better for Segui, as he proceeded to lose every one of his starts for the Mariners that year, finishing with an 0-7 record.

But there were some bright spots for Seattle. Ruppert Jones was excellent in the field and put up some impressive offensive numbers, batting .263, with 24 homers, and 76 RBIs. Another outfielder, Lee Stanton, did even better, hitting .275, with 29 home runs, and 90 RBIs.

Although the pitching was weak, Glenn Abbott picked up 12 wins. And John Montague retired 33 batters in a row in late July to tie an American League record.

The fans filled the Kingdome in that inaugural season to see their Mariners play. They usually saw a loss, but the Mariners did not finish that first year in last place, as most expansion teams do. They came close, but the Oakland Athletics occupied the cellar that year. It may not have been a great year, but by all accounts the Mariners were headed in the right direction.

Wrong Turn

The Seattle Mariners' organization and fans were excited about their second year. But the excitement didn't last long. The Mariners lost 104 games, finishing 35 games out of first place.

Leon Roberts, a new player acquired from Houston, led the offense, batting over .300, with 22 dingers, and 92 RBIs. Because Roberts was nearly the only highlight that year, attendance dropped, causing the Mariners' owners much concern.

In 1979, the Mariners improved to 67-95, good enough to keep them out of the cellar. The team was again excited about the following season.

The Mariners made some big moves and had a solid lineup going into the 1980 season. They had good pitching in Floyd Bannister, Mike Parrott, Rick Honeycutt, and in reliever Shane Rawley. The offense was led by Bruce Bochte, Willie Horton, Leon Roberts, and Tom Paciorek.

Even though there was cause for some excitement, only 22,588 fans showed up for the opener at the Kingdome in 1980. Mike Parrott got the win, as the Mariners beat the Blue Jays. Unfortunately, Parrott, the Mariners' best pitcher, would get his first and only win on opening day. He finished the season with a 1-16 record, and a whopping 7.28 ERA.

And that is how the entire season went for the Mariners. Poor playing led to another 100-loss season and a room in the cellar.

The 1981 season wasn't much better, as the Mariners continued to lose while bringing up the rear in gate receipts. Many thought that the Mariners were on the road to improvement, but somewhere along the way they took a wrong turn.

Floyd Bannister led the AL West in 1982 with 209 strikeouts.

Still Building

By 1982, the team was still building. The future looked better for the Mariners with the draft picks of pitchers Mark Langston and Mike Moore, plus outfielder Phil Bradley. The team showed signs of improvement on the field, too. They grabbed 76 victories and took fourth place in the AL West. The highlight of the season was pitcher Floyd Bannister, who led the league with 209 strikeouts.

The Mariners had a tendency to show signs of promise one season and then fall flat the following year. The 1983 season was no different. Seattle finished the year with full reign of the basement, losing a whopping 102 games. Their counterpart, the Toronto Blue Jays, were vying for the AL East crown.

Many Seattle fans believed that the 1984 season would be the turning point for this dismal franchise. There were two players who could ignite the team. Pitcher Mark Langston and first baseman Alvin Davis were teammates in the minors and came aboard as rookies for the Mariners in 1984.

Langston finished the season with 17 wins, the most ever to this point for a Mariner pitcher. Langston also had an excellent 3.40 ERA, and *The Sporting News* named him Rookie Pitcher of the Year.

Alvin Davis was a very solid-fielding first basemen, but he was better known for his bat. He finished the year with a .284 batting average, 27 homers, and 116 RBIs. For all his work he was named AL Rookie of the Year.

Besides the star rookies, the Mariners had a talented outfield in Al Cowens, Dave Henderson, and Steve Henderson. Jack Perconte, Spike Owen, and Jim Presley rounded out the infield.

The Seattle Mariners finished the 1984 season 10 games back. But because they now had a solid nucleus, they were more excited about the seasons to come.

But it wasn't to be. The 1985 season was coined "See It Happen" by the Mariners. The "it" never took place. Seattle finished 17 games out of first place. And thanks to the Texas Rangers, the Mariners just missed landing in the cellar.

Mark Langston suffered through an injury-riddled 1985. But he bounced back in 1986 with a league-leading 245 strikeouts. Rookie shortstop Danny Tartabull had a great season, smashing 25 home runs and knocking in 96 RBIs.

Jim Presley cracked 27 homers, 107 RBIs, and was named to the All-Star team. But none of this was enough, as the Mariners suffered through another losing season, and finished near the bottom.

Mariners' shortstop Danny Tartabull stretches for a ball during a game against the New York Yankees.

Now What?

The Seattle Mariners had no answers to their problems. But they didn't give up. They made some big moves before the 1987 season which turned the team around—for awhile.

Trades were this year's flavor for the Mariners. Before the 1987 season they traded Spike Owen and Dave Henderson to the Red Sox for shortstop Rey Quinones. Danny Tartabull was traded to Kansas City. Those trades neither hurt nor helped the Mariners that year, but they would haunt the Mariners in the future, as all three players went on to make a big impact in the majors.

Second baseman Harold Reynolds, who came from the Mariners' farm, led the team in steals with 60. Alvin Davis contributed his usual but impressive stats, batting .295, with 29 homers, and 100 RBIs. Mark Langston chalked up 19 wins and again led the league in strikeouts with 262.

The Mariners finished only seven games out of first place and tied for their best record ever—still not above .500. But the team was happy because they were headed in the right direction.

But as usual, the following season saw another wrong turn. The 1988 season landed the Mariners back near the bottom. The franchise wasn't even concerned about winning a pennant. First things first—they just wanted to have a winning season! But what would it take for Seattle to accomplish this? How about a kid?

The Kid

In 1989, the Mariners' luck changed when a rookie outfielder began playing for the team. This 19-year-old "kid," named Ken Griffey, Jr., was not only going to be a star, he was also going to be the franchise.

The Kid's story, however, began well before 1989. He is the son of Cincinnati Reds All-Star Ken Griffey, Sr., who was part of Cincinnati's "Big Red Machine" that won two World Series in the 1970s.

When the Kid—also known as "Junior"—was only 15 years old he went to practice with his father, who at that time was with the New York Yankees. The Kid could swing, throw, run, and catch as well as many minor leaguers. His father and the other major leagers could not believe how great a player he was.

All-Star Rickey Henderson, who was on the Yankees, knew someday that Junior would be a star in baseball, and often gave him advice. Junior idolized Henderson and listened to his advice. The Kid hoped that someday he could play in the major leagues.

That day came only four years later, on April 3, 1989, when Junior was 19 years old. Ken Griffey, Jr., punched out a double in his first

Major League Baseball at-bat. He also hit a home run in his first game in the Kingdome, and then another in his second game.

The Mariners finished the year in sixth place, but optimism was in the air. And this time it was for real.

Ken Griffey, Jr., gets a hit during 1995's ALCS against the Cleveland Indians.

Ken Griffey, Sr. (30), and his son, Ken Griffey, Jr. (24), prepare to take the field September 1, 1990. It was the first game in history where a father and son played in the same game.

The Griffeys Make History

The Mariners improved slightly in 1990, but at least they stayed on track. They added a young ace, Randy Johnson, who would become one of the best pitchers in the league. Johnson threw the first-ever Mariner no-hitter on June 2, shutting out the Detroit Tigers 2-0.

The biggest news for the Mariners, and in all of baseball, was the young Griffey playing alongside his father on the same major league team at the same time!

Ken Griffey, Sr., signed a contract in the middle of the season with the Seattle Mariners. The year before, the Griffeys made baseball history as the first father-son combination to play in the majors at the same time. The two were now making history again, playing on the same team.

On August 31, 1990, Junior and Senior played their first game together. Senior batted first and hit a smash through the middle of the infield for a single. Junior followed his father up to bat and also hit a single. The crowd went wild. Both balls were collected and taken to the Baseball Hall of Fame.

Both made it home, and scored runs that inning for the Mariners. When Junior reached the dugout after scoring, his father greeted him with a big hug.

Besides making history, the two had productive years. Senior batted .377 in 77 plate appearances. And Junior hit .300, with 22 home runs. The Kid became the first Mariner ever to be voted to start in the All-Star Game. He also won a Gold Glove Award that year.

The following season, in 1991, Junior continued to improve. He hit .327 and had 100 RBIs. He won his second-straight Gold Glove and made his second-straight start in the All-Star Game. Defensively, he was voted by the managers as the best fielding outfielder in the American League.

But the bigger news was the team's play. The Mariners, after 15 years, finally had a winning season. Seattle finished with an 83-79 record, playing .512 ball.

Young third baseman Edgar Martinez, who was being overshadowed by the Kid, had his second-straight .300 season. Led by Randy Johnson, the pitching staff was beginning to be the power in the league.

Facing page: Third baseman Edgar Martinez waits for a pitch during a game against the Kansas City Royals.

Seattle

Ruppert Jones was the first player drafted by the Seattle Mariners expansion team for their opening season in 1977.

In 1977, pitcher John Montague tied an AL record by retiring 33 batters in a row.

In 1982, Floyd Bannister struck out 209 batters, best in the AL West.

Danny Tartabull hit 25 homers in his 1986 rookie season.

Mariners

Ken Griffey, Jr., won a Gold Glove Award in 1990, then again in 1991.

Edgar Martinez won the 1995 batting title with a .356 average.

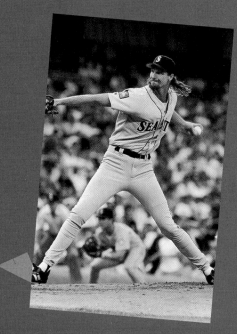

Randy Johnson picked up his fourth-straight strikeout title in 1995 with 294.

In 1995, Jay Buhner led the Mariners with 40 regular-season home runs.

What Happened?

Everything was in place for the Mariners in the 1992 season. Ken Griffey, Jr., again batted over .300. And he finished the season with 27 home runs and 103 RBIs. He made the All-Star team for the third-straight year. He had a great All-Star Game, hitting a home run, and was named the Most Valuable Player (MVP).

Edgar Martinez had another incredible year. He posted his third-consecutive .300 batting average, hitting a whopping .343 and grabbing the AL batting title—the first ever for a Mariner player.

Randy Johnson was as impressive as ever. He ran away with the strikeout title, mowing down 241 batters. Left-handed pitcher Dave Fleming led the team with 17 wins.

But for all the good things, the Mariners still lacked depth, experience, and leadership. They fell hard coming off their best season ever, finishing in the cellar for the sixth time in their short 16-year history.

The 1993 season showed some signs of improvement. Everyone knew they had some solid stars who could lead the team to a pennant in the near future.

Ken Griffey, Jr., tied a major league record by hitting home runs in eight-straight games. He finished the season again over .300, and hit 45 home runs!

Randy Johnson led the league again in strikeouts with 308. And fellow pitcher Chris Bosio threw the second no-hitter in Mariner history on April 22, as Seattle whipped the Red Sox 7-0.

Randy Johnson hurls the ball during a game against the New York Yankees.

Seattle fans were getting excited for the 1994 season, because many thought that it could finally be the year for the Mariners to grab the pennant. Both the National and American Leagues added a Central Division, making it easier to make the playoffs. But it was all for naught, as the season was canceled in August due to a players' strike.

Seattle players were having record-breaking years. Ken Griffey, Jr., picked up the home run crown, finishing the canceled season with 40. Randy Johnson picked up his third-straight strikeout title, finishing with 204. Each award was bittersweet for the players who would have much rather been playing ball. But the Mariners came back after the strike the following season—big time!

Mariners' First Pennant

The Seattle Mariners finally got their first-ever pennant in the 1995 season, due to a balanced lineup of key veterans mixed with young stars. The best young star of them all, Ken Griffey, Jr., sat out half the season due to injury. But it didn't stop the Mariners from having their greatest season in franchise history.

Capturing the pennant wasn't easy. The 1995 season saw the Seattle Mariners matching the California Angels with 78 regular-season wins. This meant a one-game playoff for the AL West crown. Seattle came out the day after the regular season ended and dominated the Angels, winning by a score of 9-1, and taking the pennant.

Throughout the regular season the Mariners played their hearts out and became the sentimental favorite for many baseball fans. Edgar Martinez again was a dominant force, playing in every single game and leading the league in three different categories. He easily grabbed the AL batting title with a .356 average. He also led the league in runs with 121, and doubles with 52. He was second in hits with 182, and finished the year with over 100 RBIs. Another Martinez, first baseman Tino, also helped with the offensive duties. He smacked 31 homers, with 111 RBIs, and hit near .300.

Jay Buhner led the Mariners with 40 home runs, placing him second behind Cleveland's Albert Belle. Veteran Vince Coleman added his leadership and a solid glove in left field. On offense he batted .288, and used his speed to steal 42 bases.

Ace pitcher Randy Johnson continued his dominance over opposing batters. Johnson had an 18-2 record on his way to picking up his fourth-straight strikeout title with 294. He also led the league with the lowest ERA of 2.48.

With the solid lineup that the Mariners had, many believed they had a chance at going to the World Series. After beating the Angels and grabbing the AL West pennant, the Mariners didn't have much time to celebrate. They immediately boarded a plane and took the long flight from Seattle to New York to play in their first-ever playoff series, matched against the Yankees.

Jay Buhner watches his hit fall for a double during a game against the Chicago White Sox.

Mike Blowers hits a two-run homer during Game 1 of the 1995 ALCS. The Mariners beat the Cleveland Indians 3-2.

In the first game of the best-of-five game series, the worn-out Mariners got beat 9-6. The next night the Yankees and Mariners fought through nine innings tied. It took an additional six innings to finally get a winner. In the bottom of the 15th inning the Yankees pulled away, winning 7-5.

The first playoff series for the Mariners was all but over. They made the long flight back to Seattle, needing a miracle. Down two games to none, the Mariners would have to win three in a row.

The Mariners got their first win of the series by a score of 7-4. The Yankees were not worried. They figured the Mariners couldn't possibly win two more. But the next night Seattle forced a fifth and deciding game by winning 11-8.

In the final game the Mariners and Yankees fought to the bitter end. After nine innings the game was tied 5-5. Finally, in the bottom of the 11th inning, the Mariners pushed across the winning run for a 6-5 victory. They were headed to the American League Championship Series (ALCS).

The Mariners had little time to celebrate their unbelievable come-from-behind victory. Two days later they would be taking on the Cleveland Indians, with the winner going to the World Series.

It was a classic matchup. Both teams were fan favorites because of the distinction of being perennial losers. Cleveland hadn't been in the playoffs for more than 40 years! And you know the Mariners' story.

If Game 1 were any indication of the flavor of the series, then it would be a thriller. The first game was in Seattle. The Mariners got off to a big start in the second inning when Mike Blowers hit a two-run homer. Cleveland came back behind a solo homer by Albert Belle. Both teams had great pitching, only allowing a run each in the seventh. Seattle picked up the early series lead one game to none.

The Indians bounced back with a 5-2 victory in Game 2, behind the pitching of Orel Hershiser and the bat of Manny Ramirez, who went 4-for-4 with 2 homers. Griffey and Buhner led the way for the Mariners, each cracking a solo home run in the losing effort.

Jay Buhner led the way for the Mariners in an 11-inning marathon, as Seattle picked up Game 3. After nine innings the game was tied at 2-2. Then in the bottom of the 11th inning with two men on, Buhner smacked his second homer of the game to give the Mariners the victory.

After that exciting third game the Mariners could only muster two more runs the rest of the series. The Indians turned it up a notch, winning the next three games and grabbing the American League pennant.

Seattle played hard from opening day to the very last game, and had a historic season.

Paul Sorrento hits a grand slam home run against the Milwaukee Brewers.

A Team On The Rise

The Seattle Mariners have suffered through some terrible seasons. But after tasting a winning season in 1991, and finally winning a pennant in 1995, they know which way they want to go.

Many times in the past they have had a good year and then have taken a wrong turn. It doesn't look as though this will happen again any time soon.

They did lose power hitters Tino Martinez and Mike Blowers. Veteran Vince Coleman also is gone, along with pitchers Andy Benes, Bill Risley, and Tim Belcher.

Newcomer Paul Sorrento will try to fill the shoes of Tino Martinez, and Russ Davis will try to fill those of Mike Blowers.

But the team will still rely heavily on Edgar Martinez, Jay Buhner, and Joey Cora for the offensive chores. And the best pitcher in the game, Randy Johnson, will still lead them from the hill.

One of the best additions to the Mariners is shortstop Alex Rodriguez. At only 21 years old, people are calling Alex the next big star in the game. After playing in only 48 games in 1995, Rodriguez became the starting shortstop in 1996. He won the AL batting crown with a .358 average. He also had 36 home runs and earned a spot on the All-Star team.

Rodriguez is 6 feet, 3 inches tall, and 195 pounds of pure grace and skill. He can run, hit, hit for power, and make all of the plays in the field. "The way he's going, someday he might bat .400 and hit 60 home runs," said Boston Red Sox General Manager Dan Duquette. "He's the best young talent I've seen in years."

And we can't forget one of the best all-around players in the league—the Kid. With Ken Griffey, Jr., on your team, you are always in the hunt come playoff time.

Glossary

All-Star: A player who is voted by fans as the best player at one position in a given year.

American League (AL): An association of baseball teams formed in 1900 which make up one-half of the major leagues.

American League Championship Series (ALCS): A best-of-seven-game playoff with the winner going to the World Series to face the National League Champions.

Batting Average: A baseball statistic calculated by dividing a batter's hits by the number of times at bat.

Earned Run Average (ERA): A baseball statistic which calculates the average number of runs a pitcher gives up per nine innings of work.

Fielding Average: A baseball statistic which calculates a fielder's success rate based on the number of chances the player has to record an out.

Hall of Fame: A memorial for the greatest baseball players of all time located in Cooperstown, New York.

Home Run (HR): A play in baseball where a batter hits the ball over the outfield fence scoring everyone on base as well as the batter.

Major Leagues: The highest ranking associations of professional baseball teams in the world, currently consisting of the American and National Baseball Leagues.

Minor Leagues: A system of professional baseball leagues at levels below Major League Baseball.

National League (NL): An association of baseball teams formed in 1876 which make up one-half of the major leagues.

National League Championship Series (NLCS): A best-of-seven-game playoff with the winner going to the World Series to face the American League Champions.

Pennant: A flag which symbolizes the championship of a professional baseball league.

Pitcher: The player on a baseball team who throws the ball for the batter to hit. The pitcher stands on a mound and pitches the ball toward the strike zone area above the plate.

Plate: The place on a baseball field where a player stands to bat. It is used to determine the width of the strike zone. Forming the point of the diamond-shaped field, it is the final goal a base runner must reach to score a run.

RBI: A baseball statistic standing for *runs batted in.* Players receive an RBI for each run that scores on their hits.

Rookie: A first-year player, especially in a professional sport.

Slugging Percentage: A statistic which points out a player's ability to hit for extra bases by taking the number of total bases hit and dividing it by the number of at bats.

Stolen Base: A play in baseball when a base runner advances to the next base while the pitcher is delivering his pitch.

Strikeout: A play in baseball when a batter is called out for failing to put the ball in play after the pitcher has delivered three strikes.

Triple Crown: A rare accomplishment when a single player finishes a season leading their league in batting average, home runs, and RBIs. A pitcher can win a Triple Crown by leading the league in wins, ERA, and strikeouts.

Walk: A play in baseball when a batter receives four pitches out of the strike zone and is allowed to go to first base.

World Series: The championship of Major League Baseball played since 1903 between the pennant winners from the American and National Leagues.

Index

A

Abbott, Glenn   9
American League (AL)   4, 6, 7, 9, 11, 12, 17, 20, 21, 22, 23, 25, 26
American League Championship Series (ALCS) 6, 25, 26
American League East   11
American League West   11, 22, 23
All-Star   12, 14, 17, 20, 28

B

Bannister, Floyd   10, 11
Belcher, Tim   27
Belle, Albert   22, 25
Benes, Andy   27
Blowers, Mike   25, 27
Bochte, Bruce   10
Bosio, Chris   20
Boston Red Sox   8, 13, 20, 28
Bradley, Phil   11
Buhner, Jay   22, 26, 27

C

California Angels   9, 22, 23
Cincinnati Reds   14
Cleveland Indians   25, 26
Coleman, Vince   22, 27
Cora, Joey   27
Cowens, Al   12

D

Davis, Alvin   11, 13
Davis, Russ   27

F

Fleming, Dave   20

G

Gold Glove Award   17
Griffey, Ken, Jr.   6, 14, 15, 17, 20, 21, 22, 26, 28
Griffey, Ken, Sr.   14

H

Hall of Fame   17
Henderson, Dave 12, 13
Henderson, Rickey 14
Henderson, Steve 12
Hershiser, Orel   26
Honeycutt, Rick   10
Horton, Willie   10

J

Johnson, Darrell 8
Johnson, Randy 6, 15, 17, 20, 21, 23, 27
Jones, Ruppert   8, 9

K

Kansas City Royals   8
Kingdome   7, 8, 9, 10, 14

L

Langston, Mark   11, 12, 13

M

Major League Baseball   7, 14
Martinez, Edgar 17, 20, 22, 27
Martinez, Tino 27
Milwaukee Brewers 7
Montague, John   9
Moore, Mike   11
Most Valuable Player (MVP) Award 20

N

New York Yankees   14, 23, 25

O

Oakland Athletics   9
Owen, Spike   12, 13

P

Pacific Coast League   7
Paciorek, Tom   10
Parrott, Mike   10
Perconte, Jack   12
Presley, Jim   12

Q

Quinones, Rey   13

R

Ramirez, Manny   26
Rawley, Shane   10
Reynolds, Harold   13
Risley, Bill   27
Roberts, Leon   10
Rodriguez, Alex   6, 28
Rookie of the Year   12

S

Seattle Pilots   7
Segui, Diego   9
Sorrento, Paul   27
Stanton, Lee   9

T

Tartabull, Danny   12, 13
Texas Rangers   12
Toronto Blue Jays   4, 6, 10, 11

W

World Series   4, 14, 23, 25